A LOVER'S LINES

DEBANGAN MAITY

Made with ♥ on the Notion Press Platform
www.notionpress.com

I want to dedicate my this book to all my readers.

success of this book depends on all of you.

Contents

A

LOVER'S

LINES

- BY

DEBANGAN MAITY

Preface

This is my first book containing few poems
serialized to tell a story , a futile love story.
If God bless then the story will be continued......

Acknowledgements

I want to thank my mother, father ,sister(DEBALINA) and my friends ,Who encourage me a lot to write this book , A Lover's Lines.

- DEBANGAN MAITY

Few Words From The Author

Hi , I'm novice writer and I write this book on behalf of a lover to request his Ladylove about his prayers.

This is a complete imaginary story that I want to tell all of you . If someone find any similarities with his

or her personal life then it's extremely coincidence and unintentionally. My intention is not to hurt anyone, if anyone gets hurt through the poems then I'm extremely sorry for this. I hope everyone , all of you will like this and share the book with others as if the message can be delivered to the Ladylove.

If God bless

the story will be continued......

-Debangan Maity

1. That Day I Saw Her !!

That day I saw her !
That day was a heavenly gifted
day to me,
That day I saw the most brightest
earthly beauty which made
me spellbound !
That day, the divine angels
were calling me from the behind
and she did act like a
connector between me and the
divine ;
That day she did put her
beautiful hand upon my
shoulder and my shoulder got
blessed with the beautiful touch
of her beautiful hand ;
That day the beautiful five fingers
of her did touch me so maidenly ,
I got mesmerized by the touch !
That day I first feel love
with a beat of my heart ,
That day I first listened the
voice of my heart ,
That day I did realize my
heart also beats ,

my heart is still living and
I'm still breathing not like
dead body but like a
human body with feelings.
That day I first got her
touch and listened that
melody full of love like
voice that pleased
my ears just like pleasing
a God by a powerful chant by
devoted priest;
That day was quite extraordinary
to me !
That day I did realize the
extraordinary movement by
the love fairy in my heart ;
her beautiful divine face
just like the moon without
any stain was pleasing my
eyes just like nature's
cold water is pleasing a
thirsty one's thirst.
That day my eyes' thirst
was fully pleased by those
divine eyes .
That day I saw her
saw her !
and just watching her
watching her !

That day I realized
my heart was captured
and I'm not the owner of
my heart; That day
the beautiful eyes, beautiful
voice and the five fingers
won my heart and awake
my soul for the first
time!
That day I saw her !
That day I saw her !
That day I saw her
Just like a day of fairy tale
where all the fairies of my
heart did suddenly start
a love melody –
and the melody Sung by
those love fairies provoked me
to love her and love her , just love
her, look her and just look at her !
The more I looked the more I loved!
It just like the time stopped
and I was falling in her eyes,
the deepness of her eyes couldn't
be measured and I just
falling and falling and falling !
It seems the journey to
infinity , the journey of
soul leaving the body and

going towards the paradise of love .
That day I saw her !
That day the thousand thunders
scattering in the sky of my heart
and the thousand drops of rain
was trying to wake up the softness
of my heart from the drought .
That day, magically, a red rose
knocking at my drought land
with her beautiful smile and
provoked me to do a journey of
love !
That day I saw her !!
That day the Psyche with an agate lamp
dropped a drop of oil to give life to
the Cupid of my heart .
That day I saw her !
That day I realized myself
for the first as a lover !
That day I saw her !

2. Her Eyes!

Her bright glittering stars
like those eyes shining
in my heart making me bound
to fall to that deep blindly;
Those beautiful dazzling hypnosis
eyes can take anyone far from
the reality to the dream world
of love where nothing is more
beautiful and mysterious than
those majestic eyes; Her eyes!
Her eyes, as clear as
The sky of Autumn;
as pleasant as
the moonlit night;
as deep as
the mysterious sea;
Her eyes just like the heavenly
image drawn by the heavenly hand
taking thousand of years
with the heavenly purity;

In those eyes God gifts
every heavenly beauty to
challenge the earthly beauty;
Every earthly beauty is just pale

in front of those heavenly eyes
just like the doom light of hell.
Those heavenly eyes just like
the full moon in the night
capture my heart with
each and every single sight !
Those heavenly pure eyes are
the doors of the mysterious world
of love where I want to be lost!
lost like a vagabond, nothing
to do except hunting the
mystery of those bright eyes..

3. Her Smile!

If moon is the most pleasant
heavenly sight in the night sky
then her Smile is the most pleasant
earthly sight in my sky.
Her Smile describes her soul's beauty
which makes me bound to love
her endlessly!!
Her Smile just like the glittering
stars and the bright half moon
shining in the night sky
that make eyes blessed.

When she smiles time stops,
earth stops, everything stop and
forget all miseries of life
and start smiling,
as if it is not the smile
of the individual one
but moreover it is the smile
of the earth, smile of the beautiful
nature.
Her smile is as beautiful
as red rose, as mist,
as first drop of rain after

the scorching heat of
the hotly summer,
beautiful as the sky of Autumn;
Oh pleasant! pleasant! that pleasant!
Her Smile!

Her smile is more beautiful
than the Helen's beauty!
even though her beautiful
smile can make Helen jealous
and the stone hearted ones
to love.
Her smile! Her smile! Her smile!
Her smile is the sun of the dawn
does erase all the darkness
of my heart and enrich
my soul to move towards her.
Whenever she smile those
red rose like kissable lips
give birth a beautiful
desire in my heart
to kiss her, kiss those lips endlessly!
and drink the nectar just like the bees!

Her beautiful smile admires
the beauty of those lips
demand a holy kiss
from a die hearted lover;

Her innocent smile provokes
me to touch those lips
and tempted me to
feel that beauty
that divine beauty!
Oh! That smile! Her smile!

4. I Wish to Kiss Her

I wish to kiss her
that'll be my first kiss!
My lips want to feel those
rosy pink lips,
like a honey bee's dream
to drink the nectar from the rose
very enthusiastically!!
I also like to drink the nectar
of those rosy lips.
The wish is not just a physical wish,
Nay! The wish is more than it.
The wish to feel her lips is just
like the wish to touch the soul.
Yes! It's my soul's wish to
Kiss her.
It's holy! as holy askissing the Bible;
It's powerful! as powerful as
Mohammad's kiss to EMAM ;

The desire isn't just a desire,
It's the need of my soul
to provide enough energy to live.
It's the need of my lips
to overcome all the miseries

to be enough fortunate.
Yes! my lips will get the divine blessing
if it able to touch those holy lips.
It's the desire to get
the blessing of God ;
It's the desire to touch that
divine beauty ;
Yes! It's holy!!
as much as the Bible ,
as much as the Ganges,
as much as the Quran.

I want to kiss her!
that will be my first!
I want to touch the world,
the world of spiritual pleasure.
Yes! I'm greedy! Very much greedy!
but I'm not ashamed
because I want to be the one
in the whole world,
I want to be the one, only one
who will be able to kiss those rosy pink lips!
This is not a physical greed ,
Yes! This is a holy greed.
Yes! This is my wish, this exactly
what I pray for, pray to God,
the almighty
to be the one, only one
to kiss her, kiss those lips endlessly!!

5. The Dream!

In a lonely, silent, stormy night
when the earth was having a sweet sleep,
my eyes were open with the thirst
to see her,
see her beauty
in that beautiful stormy night
at once!
With the open eyes I was praying to God,
"oh almighty , oh omnipotent , oh merciful,
Bless me with her affection, love and acceptance
of me; and make me pleased with her and
bring us together in the best form
of a union and in absolute harmony ".

Unknowingly my eyes were got closed
and I fall into the world of night
sleep and dream.
Suddenly I found myself into the
world where her beautiful smiley
face was glittering in front of me;
amusingly I was watching at her,
my eyes were amused! It's she,
my love, my desire, my thirst.
Her gentle face with the beautiful
Rosy smile was taking control

of the world.

She was calling me!
And I was not capable to avoid
her wild call; I started running,
chasing her all over the world!
In vain ! alas! Unfortunate!
I couldn't get her; far away
she was standing with her
maidenly attitude and smiling towards me,
"oh poor lover! try again, again and again
to catch me, your dream".
Those mesmerizing musical voice
enrich my soul to move towards
her beauty!
A scattering thunder, I woke up.
It was a dream, the first dream,
appearance of her beauty
in my unconscious world.
It was the first, the dream,
dream of a lover!

6. Dizzy Mind

Day by day you are capturing
my soul and heart but
my mind is still dizzy about you,
thousands of questions there are
with no answer
making my headache.
Are you really as gentle as I am thinking?
Are you really as pure as I am thinking?
I don't know!
maybe the reality differs!
Do you know the meaning of love?
Do you know the deepness of love?
Or
You are one of those who use
her charm and beauty to attract
the lovers and do play love games for
the crimson joy?

Or
You are one of those who do
think about the physical pleasures
and earthly things just like a
child sucker?
How are your choices my dear?

Do you see the purity of someone's heart?
Or
You just like the physical charm with
expensive gadgets and a heavy wallet?
I don't know! My dear!
Do you really want the spiritual love?
Or
all of yours wishes are still in the earthly limit?
I don't know! I don't know!
My mind is full with thousands of questions
without any answer but my heart is still beating
just for you!

But my dear my heart is beating
In favour of you,
and saying me, "you can be my bad luck
not can be my bad judgment".
Believe me my dear the pain
of bad luck is less pathetic than
the pain of bad judgment.
Be my bad luck; I will bear it
But if you be my bad judgment,
I can't able to bear it.

7. Am I Desirable??

In this time of modernity,
I am still a dull boy with very much simplicity.
And this simplicity asks me a question!
Am I desirable to you? Am I enough to
compete with your other desirers??
These questions make me afraid!
I know who I am!
I know I don't have the charm
to attract beautiful ladies and
I don't know the art of flirting to
provoke you to make love with me.

I don't have the muscular body
with a tattoo on it like others;
I also don't have those beautiful multi coloured
hair for style; I don't wear ripped
jeans to show fashion; I don't have a bike
to offer you the back seat; I am not used to
with a cigarette in between my two fingers
to show the heroic style;
I don't Speak too much; I don't have
too many friends; I am not so popular
also; I am a dull boy!

I am an old fashionable man,
I know that very well!
But I have a heart with love and honesty;
I have nothing but these two!
I know I can't compete! that's a harsh true!

I am an odd in between
those charm full men.
But ,my dear!one thing I can promise you,
that I am able to give you
a small hut with full of love
and able to protect you from every tears
till my last breath.
That's all my dear! That's all!

8. The Proposal !!

After a long futile war
between my heart and brain,
my brain was fully vanquished by the
feelings of love;
hence I decided to express my
feelings, the endless love for her
in front of her.
It was just like the preparing
for a battle, the battle to express
my eternal love towards her.
Thousands of questions coming like arrows
invaded my heart and trying to drag
myself in the world of
confusion and nervousness.
I was dragged towards the dark of fears
and asking the blessing of almighty;

A moon like love shield
Powerful as Karana's armour lightened
the dark world and enrich my soul
to express my love in front of her.
With the hope that blessings were
with me I went to her.
Suddenly thousands of soldiers

from the dark world arrived
to stop me, stop my
journey towards her.
They were taking her away,
far from me.
In that time a guardian angel took
my side to protect my love and
vanquished all soldiers of the dark.
With a thankful heart to the guardian angel
I again did start my journey to her
to express my love!

After a long travel, finally I reached
my destination , she, in front of me,
standing with thousands of glittering stars,
asked me in her maiden beautiful musical
voice, "say, what do you want to say?"
That was the time , I was waiting for;
That was the time, I was prepared for;
But alas!
The crush of the dark world
started effecting ,
I lost my voice of love.
I tried again and again!
in vain !
I couldn't get the voice back!

It was just like the chariot's wheel
of the mighty Karna;

Stuck!!
He tried again and again
but in vain!
I also tried again and again
but in vain!
It as like as the brutal destiny
destroying the valiant warrior.
Such brutality! Unimagined!
With a heavy heart I cried to
God, "oh almighty! Give me the
power, give me the words to express
my love. Oh merciful! Oh kind hearted!
let her understand my feelings ."

God answered, she answered,
"I know you love me, but alas! I have no
such feelings for you, now, I don't
want to be in a relationship, Goodbye!"
Those gentle words just like Zeus' Thunderbolt
fall on my heart and broke it into
thousands of pieces!!!
Tears, invisible tears, coming from
my eyes, I cried out in my heart,
but couldn't speak a single
word to her!
She went away!
With the heavy pain, thousands of
Pieces of my heart, I was returning
like a defeated soldier who

lost everything, his dream!
Now he has no meaning to be alive.
The life is the punishment now.

Under the unbearable pain
I, wishing to go to the dark world
of death, the guardian angel came,
hold my hand and said, " oh fool lover,
you can't get your love at once. You should try
again and again to get your love because
paradise like love can't be get too easily ".
A hope, a ray of light
awaked my soul. I started gathering
the pieces of my heart and vowed to
myself, "I will not leave her hand,
I will love her endlessly,
I will love her till the doomsday,
I will want her till my last breath."
I will try again to
win the war of love.

9. A Prayer to God

With the unendurable pain and
thousands of pieces of the broken heart
this is a orison of a lover to you,
Jehovah;
Today life is nothing but a heavy
punishment to me! Without her acceptance,
I have no desire to bear this given life.
Today I want to ask you with
my very audacity, " why? Almighty why?
Why you give me the pain?
Why you break my heart into thousands
of pieces?
If you are not able to give me my love,
then why you provoked me to love? "

"is it not funny that the omnipotent,
almighty, creator is not able to bring
my love back to me? Is it not farcical
that your, Yahweh wish is not enough
to give birth the feelings of love
in her heart for me?"
Answer me God , answer me.
With a heavy heart today this lover
taking refuge under your kind shadow
and I'm praying to you with these tears

of pain that I'm offering to you,
Please , grant my prayers, grant
my love with your noble virtues;
Lord, you are the one who can help
this lover to win the love war.
Help me as you helped every humans to
regain the paradise by sending Jesus in this earth;
Give her the feelings of love as if
she can understand my love for her.

Guide me as you guided Moses
to show the way to you,
guide her to the way of
love , to me;
God, today I need you
to win the love war
against the world of darkness;
Today, for me, order Apollo to light my
way with his brightness though
I can vanquish the world of darkness
with my eternal love for her;
Today, for me, sent the holy spirit
to hold my hand and give me
spiritual power to give birth
the feelings of love in her heart.

Today, this worshipper need you the most;
Today, time to remember your vow,
You vowed, "where is love there is God."

Do you forget your words? Lord,
If you don't forget then how? How
this die hearted lover lost his love?
God can't be defeated and your blessings
are with me, then how I lost the love war?
How I was not able to win my lover's heart?
How? Lord! How?
Forgive all the sins I have
and forgive all the audacity of mine
and help me, guide me, bless me
to win her heart and reflect yours
noble virtues again;

This is my prayers towards you, Almighty!
Just for once, for your worshipper reflect
your noble virtues again;
Reflect your kindness again.
Today I have nothing to offer you
except the thousand of pieces of my heart
and tears I have;
Accept it Lord! and bless me with
her love, her heart;
and "bring us together in the best form
of a union and in absolute harmony."

10. Love Fairy's Arrival

In answer to my prayers Guardian angel
comes from the heaven following order
of almighty to help me to reach
the world of love fairies to seek help.
The guardian guides me to
the far, thousands of miles
away from the earth to the dream
world of love fairies; There he
orders me to tell my wish
to a beautiful dancing love fairy.

Following his order I, the lover,
go to her and pray, "oh, beautiful! Dancing
love fairy! I come from far away to seek your help
with the blessing of almighty. You, dancing fairy
you know all the things." Please help me
"in the name of the father and of the
Holy spirit. Ameen."
She responds, " with the art of dancing I
Will dance and sing a love song and will
provoke her to understand your heart but
I can't make her bound; Yes! That's true!
I have the power with limitation! I can provoke
but not more than that!"

Listening her helping words
I dance in joy that at least
someone will talk to her for
me!

Thanking her with the tears
and from the core of my heart
I say, "oh beautiful! Oh dancer of love!
start your love dance and song to provoke
her to love me."
With the dazzling stars like bright
eyes she starts singing and dancing
and with her the universe also starts the
Love song , song of my heart!
Her love song reaches to my lover's
dream and she responds to the love song,
"oh beautiful fairy! Oh dazzling dancer! Please
forgive me, I can't accept your request to love him,
I have no such feelings in my heart for him neither I will
have. Tell him very rudely if he disturbs me again then I
will go to the Zeus' court and will plead to punish him.
Oh fairy! Oh dancer of the spiritual world! Please! Stop
listening his egoistic prayer. Previously I have made
it clear to him that I have no love in my heart for him.
Make peace with the rejection."

Failure again! Painful! Very painful!
Her rude rejection makes me cry. With the tears
I thanked the fairy, "Oh dancer of love! Thanks for

all your help." Now it's the time to return
to the earth with an empty hand and
unendurable pain.

Realizing my pain , both the
Guardian angel and the love fairy
order me, "Oh die hearted lover!
Propose the universe as if she is
standing in front of you, tell the universe
what you want to tell her and if your love is true
then universe will reflect your words to her."

11. The Universal Propose!

Following the order of the
Guardian angel and Love fairy,
Oh my dear! Today I, worshipper of
Your soul, admirer of your beauty, your lover,
sing a song to propose you through the
universe .
Having faith on the power of
my love and the loyalty of
universe towards the lovers
today I sing the song of
my heart;
Oh beautiful of the most beautiful!
Oh pretty of the prettiest!
Oh pure soul! Let me love your heart and
admire your eternal beauty.

This poor lover love you from
the deepest core of his
heart, understand it, my dear! and
love me in return;
I love you more than me,
I love you more than every earthly
things I have; I don't know
how and why? But the ultimate truth
Is you are the reason, you are the source

of my living body and soul;
I can climb every mountain and
Swim every ocean to get your heart;
Trust me my love and hold my hand;
Give me at least one chance to get your heart.

I vow to you, " no one can love you more than me."
I vow you , " I will protect you from every sins,
every tears, every dark till my last breath;
I will sacrifice my life just to bring that beautiful
smile on your soft, gentle, pink, rosy lips
that will shine just like a half moon
of a moonlit night in my sky."
I will admire your beauty till the
Doomsday;
I will worship your heart every
Second of my life;
I will adore each and everything
of your by taking thousand of years;
If you give me a little place in your heart
then we will take our platonic love
towards the spiritual in one beautiful night
and our soul will united having the
witness of bright moon, pleasant mist
and the holy fire.

That day our love will be eternal;
From that very day even God can't separate

our united soul and it will create
a new soul on the lap of mother earth;
And that new born will shine like
the sun in our united sky and bear
our love symbol forever; Till the end of this earth.
I know, I don't have the charm
like other men with colouring hair,
ripped jeans, earrings and a tattoo
on the muscular body with the bag
full of money; I know, I don't have
enough in my pocket to bring all
earthly pleasures to you; But
my dear, if you choose one
of those then he will adore your
physical beauty but not the spiritual,
it's mine and only my love has the power
to touch your soul!

It's I, whose love is eligible
to take a place in your heart.
Oh pure soul! Oh wise lady! Oh maiden!
Choose wisely. Ask your heart,
Your heart will definitely respond
in my favour.
After all you have all the
freedom to choose and with respect
to your freedom I can't make you
bound, I can just plead; That's all.

Last of all but not the least,
Your smile and happiness are
everything for me . If you don't
love me , no matter, I will love
you always. I will want you always
in my heart. Forever!

12. A Hope

With the enormous pain and
darkness of fear there is a hope
still in my heart dear; And that hope
causes I'm living with a smile.
A hope that one day you will
realize my love and love me
in return, one day you will tie
me within your arms and tell me
" I love you";
Those magical words will
please my soul, heal my pain
and erase all the darkness of fair
from my heart.

A hope that one day we two will
pass our time lying down on the green
grass in a beautiful garden;
A hope that one day we will
walk holding each other hands
on the road in a moonlit night;
A hope that one day we will
talk with each other all the night
till the dawn;
A hope that one day you
will wait to see me, just

to see me;

A hope that one day you
will miss me and cry for me,
saying that "I miss you";

A hope that one day you will
feel jealous watching me talking
with other ladies, that day you
will tell me very angrily, "you are
just mine, keep distance from others".
and those jealousy words will
make me smile;
A hope that one night there
will be no gap in between us
even for the air;

A hope that one day you will
come to my arms and tell
me, "I am not well, adore me
dear", and I will adore you
just like a newborn baby and
will kiss your rosy chicks;
A hope that one day we
will smile together, cry together
in each other's arms;
These are my hopes;
These hopes make me bound

to do the futile try to win
your heart;

These hopes tell me every day
that one day, one day all of
these hopes willbe true, one day
you will love me just like I do,
you will care me just like I do.
you will cry for me just like I do.
A hope in my heart that
One day,
One day,
and I wish to wait for my destiny
with the hope, maybe it is true
or false;
Only with my last breath
it can be erased from my heart,
The hope;
Hope for you!
Hope for your love!

13. The Nightmare

Having thousands of hopes in
my heart there is still dark ,
dark as a nightmare to loose you!
Believe me my dear, loosing you
is more poisonous than the Hemlock
to me!
The Nightmare makes me awake
with a sudden shutter in the
beastly dark night;
The Nightmare that one day I will see you
holding a hand, that's not mine!
And the pathetic sight will fill my eyes
with tears, tears of blood!
After the day I wish to be blind with a
wish not to see you again
holding any other's hand;

The Nightmare that one day you will be
someone else's!
That day thousands of Leeches will suck
my blood from my heart to make
it pale!

The Nightmare that one day you will

welcome an unwelcome bed!
that day I will welcome thousands
of hungry wolves in my soul
to seek the sucking pleasures
to erase the pain;
The Nightmare that one day an another
hand will touch you!
with every single touch the air
will throw a sharp harpoon towards
My heart!

The Nightmare that one day a unknown
lips will touch your lips!
That day with every single touch
my lips will kiss the Gorgon;

The Nightmare that one day your
heart will beat taking any other's
name! That day my heart will
stop by taking yours name
for the last!

14. The Destiny

The brutal beautiful destiny
is unavoidable,
We have no other option to it with disrespect
due to it's brutality we must accept;
If you and I, are destined from there
then we will be together here
just like as a beautiful heavenly pair.

We have nothing to do with it's
pain and joy,
Please dear, don't be so coy.

If it's destined that one day
you will sleep in my arms
and I will adore your beauty and charms;
If it's destined that one day
we will do nothing except
drinking nectar from each other's
lips and having the pleasure of love;

Then neither you nor me
have anything to do with disrespect,
Destiny is invincible, we must accept.

If the destiny chooses me

to dive in yours sea of beauty
then I will thank it's very generosity.

If the destiny snatches your beauty
from me then I will punish
myself with the demonic brutality.
One day destiny will send the death
to we two,
before that choose me my dear having the faith.
Death is our ultimate destiny
because we are mortal,
But even death can't touch my love
because, through these lines now it's immortal.

15. Last Few Words

These are the last few words of mine,
Want to tell you and others before draw the line;
Listen it very keenly and let your
heart be opened, and
let the mist of feelings be welcomed.

Open your heart and listen my prayer
you will find feelings of love there.
Feelings never come so easily
unless you see my heart deeply;
In that deep you will find yourself drawn
by me as if as you are mine,
Will make you realize the richness of these lines.

When the beat of your heart
will be same as mine,
I will win the love war at that time;
Don't misjudge my desperate love to you
as my ego;
Don't neglect my feelings as
a white neglects a Negro.
Don't offer your love to someone else
and don't let yourself cheated by a false;
Only my love has the purity

to match with yours,
Only my soul deserves the
soul of yours.
Look around yourself with the open heart
oh wise lady!
You'll find myself as the true worshipper
of your purity.

Last few words for the reader,
It's your responsibility to pass the message
of this lover;
If you read these lines and
tell others to read
then the lines will fulfil my very need.
Through all of you my message
will reach to my dear
and universe will bless all of you
with the love shower.
Be a holy part of the journey
of this lover
and help me to win the love war
by passing these lines one to another
and finally to her, my dear!

Love is a heavenly gifted virtue.
Love someone unconditionally.
And pray to God for that person.
If your love is pure and destined
then you will definitely get your love.

If God doesn't want then the journey will

Stop.

If God bless the story will be continued.

DEBANGAN MAITY

9 798889 865292

Printed by Libri Plureos GmbH in Hamburg,
Germany